CICCHETTI

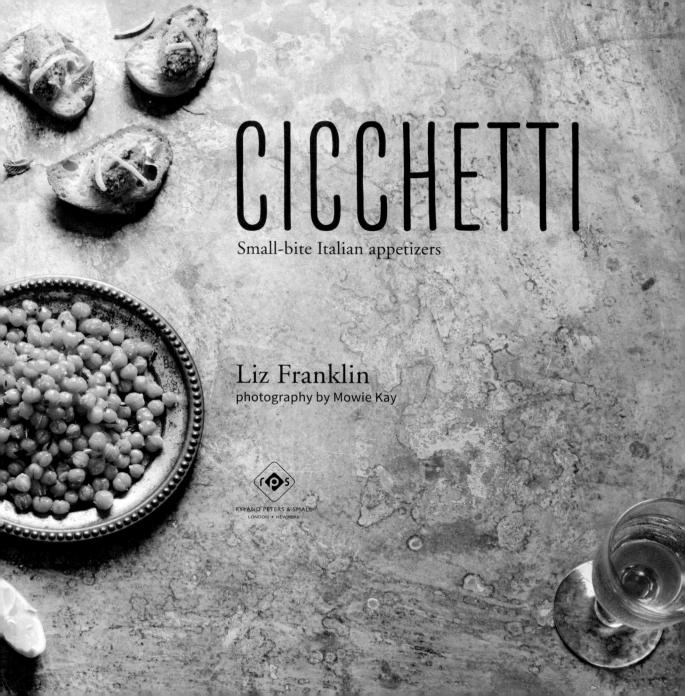

CICCHETTI

Small-bite Italian appetizers

Liz Franklin

photography by Mowie Kay

RYLAND PETERS & SMALL
LONDON • NEW YORK

This book is dedicated to my wonderful Mum and Dad, for bringing me up surrounded with love, encouragement and gorgeous things to eat – with all the love in the world.

Author's acknowledgments
With massive thanks to Julia Charles and the amazing team at Ryland Peters and Small… Megan, Patricia, Leslie, Cindy and Vanessa – for creating such a beautiful book.

A huge shout out for my editor, Stephanie Milner for her patience, professionalism and enthusiasm, and for generally being a top-notch person to work with.

Thank you so very much to Mowie Kay, for absolutely edible photography. Thank you, too, to Maud for delicious food styling and Jennifer for perfect props.

Lastly, but by no means least, thank you to my wonderful family for unconditional love and support, always. I love you xx

Senior designer Megan Smith
Commissioning editor Stephanie Milner
Production manager Gordana Simakovic
Art director Leslie Harrington
Editorial director Julia Charles
Publisher Cindy Richards

Food styling Maud Eden
Prop styling Jennifer Kay
Indexer Vanessa Bird

First published in 2016 by
Ryland Peters & Small
20–21 Jockey's Fields,
London WC1R 4BW
and
341 E 116th St,
New York NY 10029
www.rylandpeters.com

10 9 8 7 6 5 4 3 2 1

Text © Liz Franklin 2016

Design and photographs ©
Ryland Peters & Small 2016

ISBN: 978-1-84975-705-8

Printed in China

A CIP record for this book is available from the British Library.

US Library of Congress cataloging-in-publication data has been applied for.

Notes
- Both British (Metric) and American (Imperial plus US cups) are included in these recipes for your convenience, however it is important to work with one set of measurements and not alternate between the two within a recipe.
- All spoon measurements are level unless otherwise specified.
- All eggs are medium (UK) or large (US), unless specified as large, in which case US extra-large should be used. Uncooked or partially cooked eggs should not be served to the very old, frail, young children, pregnant women or those with compromised immune systems.
- Ovens should be preheated to the specified temperatures. We recommend using an oven thermometer. If using a fan-assisted oven, adjust temperatures according to the manufacturer's instructions.
- Whenever butter is called for within these recipes, unsalted butter should be used.
- When a recipe calls for the grated zest of citrus fruit, buy unwaxed fruit and wash well before using. If you can only find treated fruit, scrub well in warm soapy water before using.
- When a recipe calls for polenta, a fine cornmeal can be substituted if unavailable.

CONTENTS

INTRODUCTION

VENICE – a city of meandering canals, narrow streets, ancient squares, exquisite architecture and breathtaking beauty, rising majestically from the water. Where taxis are gondolas, buses are boats and an air of romance cloaks the entire place. The Russian writer Alexander Herzen said, 'To build a city where it is impossible to build a city is madness in itself, but to build there one of the most elegant and grandest of cities is the madness of genius'.

My first visit to Venice was with a group of friends who are food writers, and thanks to our very affable and ever-so knowledgeable tour guide William Goodacre, we were able to escape the madding crowd of tourists and discover the best sights and the most stunning food that Venice had to offer. We had a private night-time visit to the stunning Basilica di San Marco, we wandered the Jewish Ghetto, visited the Frari, saw the Bridge of Sighs from a gondola and much, much more. We sipped pre-lunch bellinis at Locanda Cipriani and feasted like superstars. We drank Prosecco at Caffè Florian, chatted over dinner at Osteria alle Testiere and filled five whole days with both cultural and edible amazement! I fell head over heels in love with Venice, a feeling that has only grown on subsequent visits.

But some of the most memorable places in which we ate weren't the high-end restaurants, famous for feeding celebrities both past and present. They were the tiny little bacari – Venetian wine bars that serve small snack-size portions of food known as cicchetti, alongside 'ombre' – equally small glasses of local wine. The name 'bacaro' comes from Bacchus, the god of wine; the name 'cicchetti' comes from the Latin 'ciccus', which means 'small' or 'modest' – and the name 'ombre' means 'shadow'… a term taken from the days when wine merchants set their barrels in the shadow of San Marco's bell tower to keep the wine from getting too warm. The places William took us to were frequented by the locals. It was the little gems we discovered then that have remained among my favourites, that have given me inspiration when entertaining and motivated me to write this book. From soft-shell crab to salt cod fritters, fritto misto and crunchy crochette, there are lots of lovely, easy-to-make treats that hopefully you will enjoy every bit as much as I do.

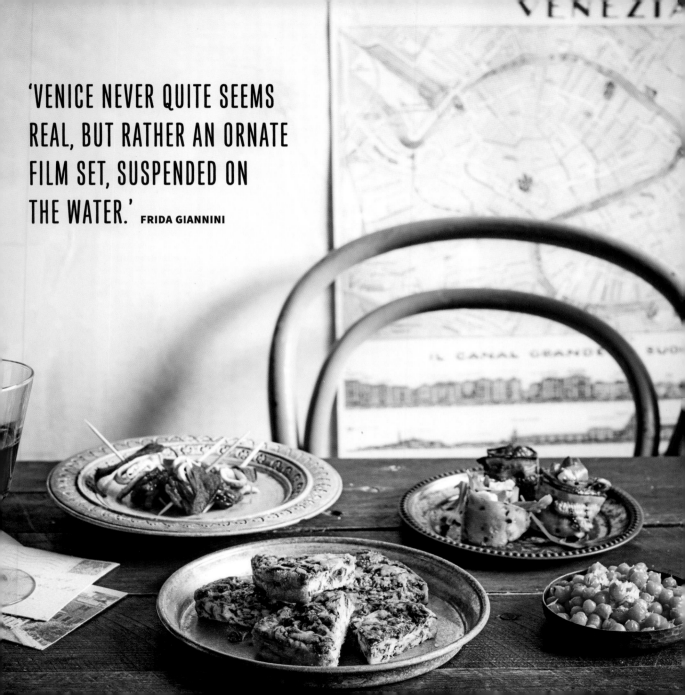

'VENICE NEVER QUITE SEEMS
REAL, BUT RATHER AN ORNATE
FILM SET, SUSPENDED ON
THE WATER.' FRIDA GIANNINI

VERDURA

VERDURA VEGETABLES

Dry-roasting chickpeas gives them a nice crunchy texture and transforms them into a tasty, healthy snack. They take an hour to dry out though, so I often put them in the oven when I am slow-roasting tomatoes to make best use of the oven.

CECI TOSTATI AL ROSMARINO
ROSEMARY ROASTED CHICKPEAS

2 x 400-g/14-oz. cans chickpeas, drained
1 tablespoon extra virgin olive oil
1 tablespoon chopped fresh rosemary
sea salt flakes, to season

SERVES 8–10

Preheat the oven to 170°C (325°F) Gas 3.

Spread the chickpeas in a single layer in a roasting dish or baking pan. Without adding anything, simply leave them in the preheated oven for an hour or so, until they are very dried out and crunchy. If you cut down the time, they'll just end up slightly crisp on the outside and still soft in the centre, and nowhere near as delicious. Be patient!

When they are crunchy, remove the chickpeas from the oven, toss in the oil and rosemary, and season with sea salt flakes.

Enjoy immediately or store in airtight container for up to 1 week.

Cipolle, or cipolline 'borettane' are small, saucer-shaped onions that come in jars, 'in agrodolce,' a sweetened vinegar that makes them incredibly addictive. I particularly like ones that are preserved in balsamic vinegar, although that does give them a dark caramel colour and you're more likely to see the pearly white ones in 'cachet' bars. Asiago is the cheese you will probably get paired with your cipolline in Venice – but when I'm home in Abruzzo I like a salty pecorino cheese. Feel free to substitute your own favourite. Don't be tempted to use ordinary pickled onions though, or, heaven forbid, the humble silverskin… they're just not the same!

FORMAGGIO VENEZIANO CON CIPOLLINE IN AGRODOLCE
VENETIAN CHEESE WITH CIPOLLINE IN AGRODOLCE

500 g/18 oz. Asiago (or other mild Italian cheese), cut into small triangles
2 x 225-g/8-oz. jars cipolline in agrodolce (pickled onions in sweet and sour brine), drained

SERVES 8–10

Top the cheese triangles with the cipolline and secure with a cocktail stick/toothpick.

Serve on a platter with drinks.

VEGETABLE ROTOLINI

Chargrilling vegetables gives them a wonderful deep, slightly smoky flavour, and when you roll them around other complementary ingredients, you have a sure-fire winner. Here are three of my favourites that make for great party food or perfect appetizers.

AUBERGINE/EGGPLANT, PESTO, TOMATOES & MOZZARELLA

20 baby plum tomatoes, halved
4–5 tablespoons extra virgin olive oil
1 long aubergine/eggplant, thinly sliced lengthways
6 tablespoons Fresh Basil Pesto (see page 14)
250 g/9 oz. buffalo mozzarella
salt and black pepper, to season

MAKES ABOUT 10

Preheat the oven to 150°C (300°F) Gas 2. Drizzle the tomatoes with a little of the oil in a roasting pan and season with salt and pepper. Cook in the preheated oven for about an hour, until they are semi-dried.

Cook the aubergine/eggplant in the same way as the courgette/zucchini (right). Season lightly and spread each length with pesto. Top with the dried tomatoes and a slice of mozzarella, and roll up to serve.

COURGETTE/ZUCCHINI, BLUE CHEESE & ROCKET/ARUGULA

3–4 courgettes/zucchini, thinly sliced lengthways
200 g/7 oz. Gorgonzola
2–3 handfuls of fresh rocket/arugula
salt and black pepper, to season
fresh basil or mint leaves, to garnish

MAKES ABOUT 16

Preheat a ridged grill pan until really hot and cook the courgette/zucchini slices on both sides, until softened, giving them a quarter turn to create a cross-hatch pattern.

When all the slices are cooked, spread with Gorgonzola. Top with rocket/arugula, season with salt and pepper, then roll up.

Transfer to a pretty serving platter, garnish with fresh basil or mint leaves and serve.

ROMANO PEPPERS, BLACK OLIVE PASTE & MOZZARELLA

3 Romano peppers
4 tablespoons black olive paste
12 anchovy fillets (optional)
250 g/9 oz. buffalo mozzarella
salt and black pepper, to season

MAKES 12

Carefully put the peppers directly over a medium flame on a gas stove and cook until the skin is blackened all over. Alternatively you could use an overhead grill/broiler. Once they are blackened all over, pop them into a plastic bag and leave to cool. The peppers should be soft and the blackened skin should come away very easily. Cut into four lengths. Season lightly and spread each length with a little olive paste. Top with an anchovy (if using) and a slice of mozzarella and roll up to serve.

Fried stuffed olives are often filled with a meat mixture that is based on the classic recipe for olives all'Ascolana (Ascolana is a region in central Italy that produces superb jumbo-size green olives with a mild flavour). Choosing a mild olive is really important – anything too astringent will spoil the balance of flavours. Here, I've gone for a lovely tomato-rich filling, softened with some ground almonds and dotted with salty speck, the wonderful cured ham from the Alto Adige region, just north of Venice.

OLIVE RIPIENE E FRITTE
FRIED STUFFED OLIVES

3–4 tablespoons extra virgin olive oil
1 white onion, finely chopped
2 garlic cloves, finely chopped
400 g/14 oz. ripe cherry tomatoes, roughly chopped
100 ml/⅓ cup plus 1 tablespoon white wine
1 teaspoon white sugar
a small handful of torn fresh basil
50 g/½ cup ground almonds
50 g/½ cup roughly chopped speck
30 jumbo-size mild green olives, pitted/stoned
3 tablespoons plain/all-purpose flour
120 g/3 cups panko breadcrumbs
salt and black pepper, to season
vegetable oil, for frying

PASTELLA
2 egg whites
60 ml/¼ cup sparkling water
60 g/½ cup self-raising/rising flour

MAKES 30

To make the filling, heat the extra virgin olive oil in a large frying pan/skillet over a low–medium heat and cook the onion and garlic for about 15 minutes, until softened but not coloured. Add the cherry tomatoes and the wine. Stir in the sugar, season with salt and black pepper, and let the mixture bubble gently for about 20 minutes. Add the torn basil, and leave to bubble for another 10 minutes or so, until the sauce is thick and sticky. If it looks a little too dry, don't be afraid to add a splash of water. Remove from the heat, stir in the ground almonds and leave to cool.

When the mixture is cold, stir in the chopped speck.

Put the mixture into a piping/pastry bag fitted with a large nozzle/tip and pipe the filling into the centre of each pitted/stoned olive.

For the pastella, beat the egg whites until light, then stir in the sparkling water. Slowly add the self-raising/rising flour and mix until smooth.

Roll the stuffed olives in the plain/all-purpose flour, dip them into the pastella and then coat in the panko breadcrumbs.

Heat the vegetable oil in a wok or deep saucepan to 190°C (375°F). Fry for 2–3 minutes, until crisp and golden.

Drain on paper towels and serve immediately.

The one slightly disappointing thing about some of the bacari in Venice is that they tend to serve their cicchetti at room temperature, unless you are lucky enough to be there when they appear from the kitchen. When I had these potatoes in the small but perfectly formed Bacaro Risorto on Campo San Provolo, close to St Mark's Square, I did think twice about ordering them, but despite not being hot, they were delicious. I guess the moral of the story is that you could serve them as a sort of potato salad, if you like – but I think they're nicer warm.

PATATE ALLA VENEZIANA
VENETIAN POTATOES

3 tablespoons extra virgin
  olive oil
30 g/2 tablespoons butter
1 medium white onion,
  finely chopped
500 g/1 lb. 2 oz. potatoes,
  peeled and diced

50 ml/3½ tablespoons
  vegetable stock
a handful of fresh flat-leaf
  parsley, finely chopped

SERVES 6

Put the oil and butter into a frying pan/skillet over a medium heat and cook the onion until softened but not coloured. Add the potatoes and stir. Reduce the heat slightly. Cook for 5 minutes, then add the stock. Continue to cook over a low–medium heat, stirring gently now and again, until the potatoes are cooked through (adding a little more stock if necessary).

Stir in the chopped parsley, season with salt and pepper, and serve.

I have more than a handful of friends who swore they didn't like polenta until they tasted these crispy, golden 'fries', given some oomph with well-flavoured stock and lots of Parmesan cheese!

CHIPS CROCCANTI DI POLENTA CON PESTO
POLENTA FRIES WITH PESTO

500 ml/2 cups good-
  quality stock
125 g/¾ cup fine quick-
  cook polenta
30 g/2 tablespoons butter
50 g/⅔ cup finely grated
  Parmesan
sunflower oil, for frying

baking sheet, oiled

SERVES 6

FRESH BASIL PESTO
2 large handfuls of fresh
  basil leaves
2 garlic cloves
120 ml/½ cup extra virgin
  olive oil
zest of 1 lemon and juice
  of ½
50 g/⅔ cup finely grated
  Parmesan
sea salt flakes, to season

Bring the stock to a boil in a saucepan, turn the heat down and slowly add the polenta, stirring all the time. Stir until the polenta is thick and smooth and comes away from the sides of the pan. Remove from the heat and stir in the butter and Parmesan. Spread the polenta onto the prepared baking sheet to a depth of about 1 cm/⅜ inch. Leave to set and when completely cold, cut into 'fries' using a sharp knife.

To make the pesto, put the basil, garlic and oil into a food processor and whizz. Add the lemon zest, juice and Parmesan. Whizz again and season.

Pour the sunflower oil into a deep saucepan and heat to 190°C (375°F). Fry the fries until golden and crisp. Drain on paper towels and serve immediately.

This is my adaptation of a simple cicchetto I had at the wonderful Cantina Do Mori on the Calle dei Do Mori near the Rialto market. It's a lovely place – all dark wood and hanging copper cauldrons and supposedly the oldest Bacari in Venice. Baby aubergines/eggplant are perfect for this, and look so pretty – but if you can't get hold of them, simply choose one that is longer rather than very round.

CANAPÈ DI MELANZANE E POMODORI
AUBERGINE/EGGPLANT & TOMATO TOOTHPICKS

10 baby aubergines/eggplant
    (or 1 long, thin aubergine/eggplant)
3 tablespoons extra virgin olive oil
1 tablespoon fresh thyme leaves
2 tablespoons finely grated Parmesan
20 bocconcini (small mozzarella balls)
salt and black pepper, to season
fresh basil leaves, to garnish

TOMATO SAUCE
3–4 tablespoons extra virgin olive oil
1 white onion, finely chopped
2 garlic cloves, finely chopped
400 g/14 oz. ripe cherry tomatoes,
    halved
100 ml/⅓ cup plus 1 tablespoon
    white wine
1 teaspoon white sugar
a small handful of torn fresh basil

MAKES 20

Preheat the oven to 190°C (375°F) Gas 5.

If you are using baby aubergines/eggplant, simply cut them in half. If you are using a large aubergine/eggplant, cut it in half lengthways, then into wedges that create small 'boats'. You will have to cut a little from the top of each wedge to create a flat surface. Score the surface without the skin of each with a criss-cross pattern.

Brush the aubergine/eggplant with extra virgin olive oil, season with salt and pepper, scatter with thyme leaves, then sprinkle over the Parmesan. Arrange on a baking sheet and cook in the preheated oven for about 20 minutes or so, until the aubergine/eggplant is soft and the skin is crisp.

Meanwhile, make the tomato sauce. Heat the oil in a large frying pan/skillet over a low–medium heat and cook the onion and garlic for about 15 minutes, until softened but not coloured. Add the cherry tomatoes and the wine. Stir in the sugar, season with salt and pepper and let the mixture bubble gently for about 20 minutes. Add the torn basil, and leave to bubble for another 10 minutes or so, until the sauce is thick and sticky.

Spoon a little of the sauce onto each piece of aubergine/eggplant, top with a bocconcini ball and garnish with a small basil leaf, securing everything with a cocktail stick/toothpick. Serve immediately.

Figs have a natural affinity with blue cheese, and the rocket/ arugula balances the sweet and the salt with a peppery kick. I like to smear the pizzette bases with a layer of Robiolino – a lovely soft, mild cheese not unlike Philadelphia but with a slightly less pronounced flavour. Choose figs that are ripe, but not too soft. My pizzette base requires a little time to make – but I promise it's worth it!

PIZZETTE DI FICHI, FORMAGGIO E RUCOLA
FIG, BLUE CHEESE & ROCKET/ARUGULA PIZZETTE

300 g/10½ oz. Robiolino
   (or other buttery cream cheese)
400 g/14 oz. Gorgonzola
4–5 ripe fresh figs
a generous handful of fresh
   rocket/arugula

PIZZETTE DOUGH
500 g/3¾ cups Italian '00' flour
10 g/2 teaspoons salt
5 g/1 teaspoon fresh yeast
250 ml/1 cup warm water

MARGHERITA PIZZETTE (OPTIONAL)
120 ml/4 oz. passata/strained
   tomatoes
½ teaspoon dried oregano
1 tablespoon extra virgin olive oil,
   plus extra to drizzle
400 g/14 oz. buffalo mozzarella
fresh basil leaves, to garnish

3 large baking sheets, floured

MAKES 8

First, prepare the pizzette dough. Put the flour into a large mixing bowl and stir in the salt. In a separate bowl, stir the yeast and water together until the yeast has dissolved and then mix it into the flour. Bring everything together to form a soft dough. Leave the mixture to rest for 10 minutes, then lightly knead the dough, cover and leave to rest for 1 hour, somewhere not too warm. Lightly knead the dough a second time and leave for a further 1 hour. Knead the dough a third time, then cut into 8 pieces. Roll the dough out into 20-cm/8-inch circles, making sure the bases are really thin. Lay them on the prepared baking sheets and leave for 30 minutes while you preheat the oven to its highest setting, usually 230°C (450°F) Gas 8.

Spread the bases with a thin layer of Robiolino. Arrange small nuggets of Gorgonzola evenly over the top and bake for 8–10 minutes, until the bases are crisp and golden. Slice or quarter the fresh figs and arrange them over the pizzette. Garnish with fresh rocket/arugula and serve immediately.

MARGHERITA PIZZETTE
Prepare the bases as above, mix the passata/strained tomatoes, oregano and oil together, and spread a thin layer over each base. Tear the mozzarella into pieces and arrange over each pizzette. Drizzle with olive oil and bake as above. Garnish with fresh basil leaves and serve immediately.

If I'm perfectly honest, I had neither these crochette, nor the chilli/chile jam I've paired them with anywhere in Venice. I did have some quite delightful, crisp fluffy crocchette – but I couldn't resist offering up a version that combines the fresh flavour of courgettes/zucchini with rich Parmesan cheese to dip into a sweet and spicy sauce. They are simply delicious!

CROCCHETTE DI ZUCCHINE E PARMIGIANO
COURGETTE/ZUCCHINI & PARMESAN CROCCHETTE

200 g/7 oz. courgettes/zucchini,
  coarsely grated
1 teaspoon salt
500 g/1 lb. 2 oz. potatoes, scrubbed
  clean but not peeled
100 g/1½ cups finely grated
  Parmesan
1 egg, beaten
120 g/3 cups panko breadcrumbs
black pepper, to season
sunflower oil, for frying

CHILLI/CHILE JAM
1 kg/2 lbs. 3 oz. ripe tomatoes
8 fresh red chillies/chiles
3-cm/1¼-inch piece of fresh ginger,
  grated
100 ml/⅓ cup plus 1 tablespoon
  white wine vinegar
250 g/1¼ cups caster/granulated
  sugar
2 tablespoons extra virgin olive oil

sterilized glass jars

MAKES ABOUT 12

First put the grated courgettes/zucchini into a colander or large sieve/strainer and sprinkle over the salt. Leave for 30 minutes or so, until they start to ooze water. Squeeze as much liquid as possible out of them (or else you'll have sloppy croquettes!) and set aside.

Boil the potatoes in a large saucepan of salted water, until they are soft all the way through when tested with a metal skewer or the thin blade of a knife. Drain and leave until cold enough to handle comfortably.

To make the chilli/chile jam, whizz the tomatoes and chillies/chiles to a purée in a food processor or blender. Transfer the mixture to a large saucepan and add the ginger, vinegar and sugar. Cook over a low heat until the sugar has dissolved, and then bubble for 30 minutes or so, until the mixture has reduced and thickened. Add the extra virgin olive oil and cook for another 15 minutes or so, until the mixture has the consistency of jam. Store in sterilized glass jars until ready to use.

Peel the potatoes and coarsely grate them into a large bowl. Add the grated courgettes/zucchini and Parmesan, and stir in the beaten egg. Add a good grind of black pepper to season and form the mixture into small log shapes. Roll lightly in the panko breadcrumbs and set aside.

Heat the sunflower oil in a deep saucepan to 190°C (375°F). Fry the crochette until golden. Drain on paper towels and serve with the chilli/chile jam.

If you stick to the poorer quality cicchetti bars in Venice, sadly it's actually possible to eat your own body weight in batter. But thanks to wonderful little bacari such as Cantina Do Mori, it's also very possible to get lots of lovely fresh veg in, too, and these delightful little saucer-sized frittate are the perfect example. I make them in my non-stick mini wok on the stove, but you could make them in very small, lightly oiled cake pans, or even make one large frittata and cut it neatly into squares or triangles. I use spinach and herbs here, but you can vary the veggies and even add some grated cheese.

FRITTATE DI SPINACI FRESCHI E ERBE AROMATICHE
FRESH SPINACH & HERB FRITTATE

a large handful of fresh spinach
4–5 tablespoons extra virgin olive oil
1 small onion, finely chopped
6 eggs, beaten
a handful of mixed fresh herbs (I like
    flat-leaf parsley, basil and chives),
    finely chopped
salt and black pepper, to season

MAKES 3 MINI FRITTATE

Wash the spinach thoroughly and squeeze lightly to remove excess water. Cook the spinach in a small saucepan over a medium heat until it is wilted – this should only take 2–3 minutes. Set aside to cool, and then chop well.

Heat 2 tablespoons of the oil in a small frying pan/skillet and cook the onion until it is soft but still translucent. Leave it to cool a little and then add it to the spinach and mix well. Add the beaten eggs and mix well. Season to taste with salt and pepper, then stir in the chopped herbs.

Add a little of the remaining oil to a very small omelette pan or mini wok set over a medium heat and pour in one-third of the mixture. Using a non-stick spoon or spatula, draw the egg mixture from the sides of the pan into the middle, until the whole frittata begins to set. Turn the heat down to low and let the frittata continue to cook until completely set (I sometimes flip it over at this stage).

When fully set, remove the pan from the heat and keep warm. Repeat with the remaining mixture. If preferred, you could preheat the oven to 180°C (350°F) Gas 4 and divide the mixture between three small saucer-size cake pans, and cook for about 20 minutes, until set. Or alternatively pour the whole lot into a roasting pan and cook for about 30 minutes.

Cut into slices or squares and serve warm.

Arancini are little golden balls of delight made from left-over risotto, usually with a little cheese or meat ragù hidden in the centre. I empathise totally with Russell Norman, when he says in his lovely Polpo cookbook that he doesn't understand the concept of leftover risotto, so I've included the recipe for a delicious one here. Mozzarella is the cheese most often used in the centre of arancini, but I use Asiago – a lovely cheese from the Veneto region that has DOP certification. I think the result is lighter and lovelier than the arancini I've enjoyed to date – I hope you'll agree!

ARANCINI DI ROSMARINO E ASIAGO
ROSEMARY & ASIAGO ARANCINI

800–850 ml/3¼–3½ cups good-quality vegetable stock
3 tablespoons extra virgin olive oil
1 onion, chopped
70 g/4½ tablespoons butter
400 g/2½ cups carnaroli risotto rice
120 ml/½ cup white wine
100 g/1½ cups finely grated Parmesan
2 tablespoons finely chopped fresh rosemary
200 g/7 oz. Asiago (or other mild Italian cheese), cut into 1-cm/ ⅜-inch cubes
50 g/⅓ cups fine quick-cook polenta (I use Polenta Valsugana)
1 litre/quart sunflower oil, for frying

PASTELLA
1 egg white
30 ml/2 tablespoons sparkling water
30 g/⅓ cup self-raising/rising flour

MAKES ABOUT 24

To make the risotto, heat the stock in a saucepan until very hot but not boiling. Heat the extra virgin olive oil in a frying pan/skillet over a low–medium heat and sauté the onion gently for 10 minutes or so, until soft but not coloured. Add 20 g/1⅓ tablespoons of the butter to the pan and pour in the rice. Stir gently until all the rice grains are shiny and coated in butter. Add the wine, and stir until it has been absorbed. Add the stock, a ladle at a time, stirring gently in between each addition, until the rice is cooked and the stock has all been absorbed. Stir in the remaining butter, the Parmesan and the chopped rosemary. Leave the risotto until completely cold. It helps to make the risotto several hours in advance, or even the day before – you can speed up the cooling process by spreading the risotto onto a baking sheet.

To make the pastella, whisk the egg white, stir in the sparkling water, then add the flour and stir until the mixture is smooth.

Form the rice into balls the size of a large walnut, and push a cube of Asiago cheese into the centre of each one. Roll the arancini in the pastella, then coat lightly with the polenta.

Heat the oil in a deep saucepan to 190°C (375°F) and fry the arancini for 2–3 minutes, until golden. Drain on paper towels and serve immediately.

PESCE

I've lost count of the times I've eaten mixed fried fish in Italy. Each region has its own version — be that battered, crumbed or simply floured and fried. The fritto misto at the Ristorante Quadri in Venice is the best I've ever had. To recreate its crunchy light coating, I use a flour called 'semola rimacinata', a double-milled durum wheat flour, but a mixture of Italian '00' flour and fine polenta makes an acceptable substitute.

FRITTO MISTO DI PESCE
MIXED FRIED FISH

1 kg/2 lbs. 3 oz. mixed fish, such as fresh anchovies, whitebait, shell-on prawns/shrimp, baby squid
2 egg whites
200 ml/¾ cup sparkling water
1 litre/quart sunflower oil, for frying
3 tablespoons plain/all-purpose flour
180 g/1¼ cups Italian 'semola rimacinata' (or 100 g/¾ cup Italian '00' flour mixed with 80 g/½ cup fine quick-cook polenta)
sea salt flakes, to season
lemon wedges, to serve

SEAFOOD SAUCE
1 egg
juice of ½ lemon
1 garlic clove, chopped
1 generous teaspoon Dijon mustard
200 ml/¾ cup sunflower oil
100 ml/⅓ cup extra virgin olive oil
4 tablespoons tomato ketchup
dried chilli/hot red pepper flakes, to taste

SERVES 4

First, make the seafood sauce. Put the egg, lemon juice, garlic and mustard into the bowl of a blender. Whizz to combine. With the motor running, slowly drizzle in the sunflower oil, until the mixture starts to thicken. Drizzle in the extra virgin olive oil, until the mixture is thick and both oils have been incorporated. Add the ketchup and a pinch of dried chilli/hot red pepper flakes and stir to combine. Refrigerate until ready to use.

Clean the fish and cut the squid bodies (if using) into rings.

Beat the egg whites until smooth and then stir in the sparkling water.

Preheat the oil in a deep saucepan to 190°C (375°F).

Dust the fish in the plain/all-purpose flour, dip it into the whisked egg mixture and then into the semola remacinata (or flour and polenta mixture). Fry the fish in the oil for 2–3 minutes, until golden, taking care not to crowd the pan.

Drain on paper towels and serve immediately, sprinkled with salt and with lemon wedges and seafood sauce on the side.

I find it hard to resist skewers of glistening marinated baby octopus. Serve with a simple caper and lemon mayonnaise to dip into – delish!

SPIEDINI DI MOSCARDINI MARINATI
MARINATED BABY OCTOPUS

500 g/1 lb. 2 oz. baby
    octopus (or baby squid)
100 ml/⅓ cup plus
    1 tablespoon extra
    virgin olive oil
zest and juice of 2 lemons
½ teaspoon paprika
a pinch of dried chilli/hot
    red pepper flakes

1 teaspoon caster/
    granulated sugar
1 garlic clove, finely
    chopped
salt and black pepper,
    to season
fresh flat-leaf parsley,
    chopped, to garnish

SERVES 4

Bring a large pan of salted to water to the boil and drop in the baby octopus. Cook for 25 minutes or so, until tender. If you are using baby squid, you could cook them simply for just 4–5 minutes. Drain and transfer to a large bowl.

Meanwhile, mix the oil, lemon zest and juice, paprika, chilli/hot red pepper flakes, sugar and garlic until well combined and season to taste with salt and pepper. Pour the dressing over the warm octopus (or squid) and leave to cool.

Thread them onto wooden skewers and arrange on a platter. Spoon over the marinade and garnish with fresh parsley.

Of all the bars in Venice, Harry's Bar is undoubtedly the most legendary. Famed for its association with Hemingway and acknowledged as the birthplace of the Bellini (see page 62), it is also responsible for putting carpaccio on the world's culinary map. The original was a dish based on wafer thin slices of beef fillet, but 'carpaccio' has come to describe thinly sliced anything. I adore this dish. It is lemony and light, and the perfect foil to all things fried!

CARPACCIO DI PESCE
FRESH FISH CARPACCIO

750 g/1⅔ lbs. very fresh
    fish, skinned and
    pin-boned
2½ lemons
100 ml/generous ⅓ cup
    extra virgin olive oil

1 teaspoon caster/
    granulated sugar
2 tablespoons capers
a handful of rocket/arugula
sea salt flakes and black
    pepper, to season

SERVES 4-6

Cut the fish into very thin slices, at an angle (as if you were slicing smoked salmon from a whole fillet) and lay the slices out on a pretty platter. Squeeze over the juice of around half a lemon and season the fish with sea salt flakes. Leave for 10–15 minutes, until the fish begins to turn opaque.

Whisk the oil with the zest and juice of 2 lemons and stir in the sugar. Pour the mixture evenly over the fish and scatter over the capers. Add a light grinding of black pepper and leave for another 10–15 minutes.

Scatter with fresh rocket/arugula and serve.

Baby plum tomatoes are best here, rather than cherry tomatoes. Long, slow cooking is best, too, so you could cook overnight on a very low heat setting. Please take the quantity as a rough guide – if you're anything like me, half of them may not make it past your mouth and you'll only have to start again…

POMODORI SECCHI FATTI IN CASA CON ACCIUGHE FRESCHE E SALVIA FRITTA
DRIED TOMATOES, FRESH ANCHOVIES & SIZZLED SAGE

1 kg/2 lbs. 3 oz. baby plum tomatoes, halved
3 tablespoons extra virgin olive oil
1 tablespoon white sugar
a handful of fresh young sage leaves

150 g/5 oz. marinated (white) anchovies
salt and black pepper, to season
sunflower oil, for frying

MAKES ABOUT 30

Preheat the oven to 170°C (325°F) Gas 3.

Arrange the tomatoes in a single layer on baking sheets. Drizzle with extra virgin olive oil and scatter over the sugar. Season with salt and pepper and bake in the preheated oven for a couple of hours (or overnight on the lowest heat setting), until sticky.

Heat the sunflower oil in a wok or saucepan to 190°C (375°F) and fry the sage leaves for a few seconds until crisp and golden. Drain on paper towels.

Arrange little stacks of tomatoes and top with an anchovy and a sizzled sage leaf. Secure with a cocktail stick/toothpick and serve at once.

I've always had a soft spot for griddled squid tentacles doused in Thai dressing, but when I had them fried until crisp, arranged on wooden skewers and served in a brown paper cone at the Cantina Do Spade, I fell in love with them all over again. These make a fun food offering for a party.

SPIEDINI DI TENTACOLI DI CALAMARO FRITTI
CRISP SQUID TENTACLES ON SKEWERS

60 g/½ cup plain/all-purpose flour (I use Italian '00' flour)
40 g/⅓ cup fine quick-cook polenta (I use Polenta Valsugana)

300 g/10½ oz. squid tentacles, cleaned
150 ml/⅔ cup whole milk
vegetable oil, for frying
sea salt flakes, to season
lemon wedges, to serve

SERVES 4

Mix the flour and polenta together in a mixing bowl.

Heat the vegetable oil in a large saucepan or wok to 190°C (375°F).

Dip the squid tentacles into the milk and roll in the flour mixture.

Fry for 2–3 minutes, until crisp and golden. Drain on paper towels and thread onto skewers. Serve in paper cones sprinkled with sea salt flakes and with wedges of fresh lemon on the side.

All over Italy, it's quite common to find a seafood salad on the menu. Some are freshly prepared. Some are bought in. You can buy frozen mixed fish for seafood salads, but I think it's best avoided, and you don't need all manner of unrecognisable things in the mix, which is often what you get. Just stick to simple shellfish – some juicy fat prawns/shrimp, perhaps a little griddled baby squid – and that's all.

INSALATA DI FRUTTI DI MARE
SEAFOOD SALAD

6–7 tablespoons extra virgin olive oil

3 shallots, peeled and finely chopped

2 garlic cloves, chopped

1 kg/2 lbs. 3 oz. mixed shellfish, such as mussels, clams, razor clams, cleaned and debearded

100 ml/generous ⅓ cup white wine

12–15 shell-on jumbo prawns/shrimp

8–10 baby squid

150 g/5½ oz. cherry tomatoes, roughly chopped

lemon wedges and crusty bread, to serve

DRESSING

200 ml/¾ cup extra virgin olive oil

2 tablespoons red wine vinegar

zest and juice of 2 lemons

2 garlic cloves, chopped

1–2 teaspoons caster/granulated sugar

a large handful of fresh flat-leaf parsley, chopped

½ teaspoon dried chilli/hot red pepper flakes (optional)

SERVES 6–8 AS PART OF A SELECTION

Heat 4 tablespoons of the extra virgin olive oil in a large saucepan and add the shallots and garlic. Cook over a low–medium heat for 5–6 minutes, until softened. Turn up the heat. Add the mixed shellfish and pour in the white wine. Cover with a lid and cook until the shells are all open. Remove from the pan and save the cooking liquor. Remove the shells from the mussels and clams, discarding any that have stayed closed. If you are using razor clams, leave the shells on – if you are using vongole veraci, remove the shells from around half of them.

Bring a large saucepan of salted water to the boil. Drop in the prawns/shrimp and cook for 3–4 minutes, until they have turned completely pink. Don't overcook them or you'll have something that resembles cotton wool rather than nice juicy prawns/shrimp. Remove from the pan and leave until cool enough to handle. Remove the shells from all but a few of them and devein. Add to the bowl with the mixed shellfish.

Preheat a griddle pan until very hot, brush the squid with the remaining extra virgin olive oil and cook for 2–3 minutes, until just opaque. Cut them in half (if you're using calamari, cut into small pieces and score with a diamond shape before griddling) and add them to the bowl with the other seafood. Gently stir in the tomatoes.

Mix all the ingredients for the dressing together, add some of the reserved cooking liquor to taste, and pour the mixture over the seafood. Leave for 30 minutes to marinate and serve with lemon wedges and crusty bread.

Little soft-shell crabs known as 'moeche' appear in the markets and restaurants of Venice for only a tiny window each year. It's not that they suddenly appear in the lagoon – it's that they are shedding their shells in preparation for new ones, and for a short time are 'without armour' as the Italians say. They are dropped live, into a Parmesan-rich batter – which they gobble up until they meet their cheesy ending. Death by batter. In the area of Italy where I have my house, we have more readily available little crabs known as 'granchietti' whose shells and pincers can be removed.

MOECA CON MAIONESE DI CAPPERI E LIMONE
SOFT-SHELL CRAB WITH FRESH LEMON & CAPER MAYONNAISE

24 soft-shell crabs
400 ml/1⅔ cups sparkling water
2 eggs, beaten
200 g/1½ cups self-raising/rising flour
80 g/1¼ cups finely grated Parmesan
finely grated zest of 1 lemon
salt, to season
1 litre/quart sunflower oil, for frying
lemon wedges, to serve

LEMON & CAPER MAYONNAISE
1 egg
1 tablespoon Dijon mustard
1 tablespoon white wine vinegar
salt, to season
300 ml/1¼ cups sunflower oil
2 tablespoons capers, rinsed and drained
zest of 1 lemon and juice of ½, to taste

MAKES 24

Make the caper mayonnaise first. Don't use eggs that have come straight out of the fridge as they won't emulsify. Put the egg, mustard and vinegar into the bowl of a blender. Add a little salt to season. Put the lid of the blender on and, with the motor running, slowly trickle in the oil. As the mixture starts to thicken, you can add the oil a little more quickly. When all the oil is fully incorporated and the mixture is thick, stir in the capers and lemon zest. Add fresh lemon juice to taste and refrigerate until ready to use.

Pull the shells gently but firmly from the crabs. Break off the larger front pincers and discard them.

Pour the sparkling water into a large bowl and beat in the eggs. Slowly add the flour and whisk until smooth. Add the Parmesan and lemon zest and season lightly with a little salt.

Heat the oil in a large saucepan or wok to 190°C (375°F). Dip the crabs into the batter and fry them for 3–4 minutes, until the batter is crisp and golden. Drain on paper towels and serve with lemon wedges and the lemon and caper mayonnaise.

I love the way Saor, the classic Venetian sweet and sour sauce, transforms sardines into something really special, and so I thought I would give it a go with one of my favourite species of fish – red mullet. I was rather pleased that I did! I serve this as a standalone dish, rather than on crostini as the city's traditional sardines in saor are typically presented. It makes a really pretty appetizer, with a crisp salad and crusty bread. Adding a few fennel seeds to the onions gives a deliciously different touch, too.

TRIGLIE IN SAOR
RED MULLET IN SAOR

12 red mullet (on the small side of medium), filleted
6 tablespoons extra virgin olive oil
3 onions, thinly sliced
400 ml/1⅔ cups white wine vinegar
125 g/1 cup sultanas/golden raisins
1 teaspoon fennel seeds
1 tablespoon dark runny honey (I like chestnut honey)
sea salt flakes, to season
1–2 tablespoons toasted pine nuts, to serve

SERVES 4

Remove the tiny pin bones from the red mullet fillets using a pair of fish tweezers and a little patience. Set aside.

Pour 5 tablespoons of the oil into a large frying pan/skillet and add the onions. Cook over a low heat for about 20 minutes or so, until they start to soften, but don't let them brown.

Pour in the white wine vinegar and turn the heat up. Bubble over a fairly high heat for about 5 minutes, then add the sultanas/golden raisins and fennel seeds. Turn the heat down and cook for a further 10–15 minutes. Stir in the honey and season with sea salt flakes.

Meanwhile, brush the red mullet fillets with the remaining oil and cook, skin-side down, for a minute or so. Turn the fillets over and cook for a further 2 minutes. Season with salt if necessary.

Layer the onions and fish in a non-metallic container and leave in the fridge overnight. Remove from the fridge half an hour before serving. Arrange on a pretty platter, scatter with toasted pine nuts and serve.

If you buy scallops in their shells, then you have readymade little serving dishes. If you buy the scallops already out of their shell, many fishmongers sell the shells quite cheaply anyway (or sometimes kitchen shops have them). You can wash the shells and re-use them time and time again. Whatever you do, please don't buy frozen scallops.

CAPESANTE E FAGIOLI BORLOTTI
SCALLOPS WITH BORLOTTI BEANS

12 scallops, cleaned and coral removed
2–3 tablespoons extra virgin olive oil
1 teaspoon mild curry powder
lemon wedges, to serve (optional)

BORLOTTI BEANS
1 x 300-g/10½ oz. canned borlotti beans, drained
½ stick/rib celery, finely chopped
¼ small fennel bulb, finely chopped
50 ml/3½ tablespoons extra virgin olive oil
1 garlic clove, finely chopped
zest and juice of 1 lemon
a pinch of caster/granulated sugar
a handful of fresh flat-leaf parsley, finely chopped
salt and black pepper, to season

MAKES 12

Brush the scallops with extra virgin olive oil and dust lightly with curry powder. Brush a frying pan/skillet with a further tablespoon of oil and set over a high heat. Fry the scallops for 2 minutes. Turn them over and fry for a further minute.

For the borlotti beans, put the drained beans into a large mixing bowl. Add the celery and fennel. In a separate bowl, whisk the oil, garlic, lemon zest and juice together with the sugar until well mixed. Pour the dressing over the bean mixture, stir in the parsley and season with salt and pepper.

Divide the beans between the scallop shells or bowls and top each with a scallop. Serve immediately with extra lemon wedges, if desired, to squeeze over.

CARNE

This is another yummy dish based on something I ate at Osteria Alla Ciurma in the San Polo district, but I have to admit to cheating here and using the whole baby artichoke hearts that come in jars 'sottolio' (under oil), rather than preparing fresh ones from scratch. It makes them much quicker to rustle up, although if you have a glut of fresh artichokes, simply prepare them in the usual way and cook them in boiling salted water until soft.

CARCIOFI CON TALEGGIO E PROSCIUTTO
ARTICHOKES WITH TALEGGIO CHEESE & PROSCIUTTO

8 whole baby artichokes in oil, drained
160 g/5½ oz. Taleggio cheese
8 slices prosciutto ham
1 litre/quart sunflower oil, for deep-frying
3 tablespoons plain/all-purpose flour, for dusting
fresh lemon juice and sea salt flakes, to serve

PASTELLA
1 egg white, beaten
130 ml/½ cup sparkling water
100 g/¾ cup self-raising/rising flour
salt, to season
zest of 1 lemon

MAKES 16

Remove the artichokes from the oil and dry them on paper towels. Gently make a hole in the centre of each one using a teaspoon or little finger. Push a small amount of Taleggio into the hole. Wrap each artichoke with a slice of prosciutto and set aside.

To make the pastella, whisk the egg white and sparkling water together. Slowly add the self-raising/rising flour and beat until smooth. Season with salt and stir in the lemon zest.

Dust the prepared artichokes in the plain/all-purpose flour and shake off any excess.

Heat the sunflower oil in a wok or deep saucepan to 190°C (375°F). Dip the floured artichokes into the pastella and deep-fry for 3–4 minutes, until golden and crisp. Drain on paper towels.

Squeeze over some fresh lemon juice, add a scattering of sea salt flakes, slice in half and serve immediately.

Simple, but delicious. Artichokes in olive oil are much nicer than the cheaper ones that come in sunflower or vegetable oil. Similarly simple to the Aubergine/Eggplant and Tomato Toothpicks on page 17, these make a nice change to fried cicchetti.

CARCIOFI E PROSCIUTTO
ARTICHOKES WITH PROSCIUTTO

1 x 190-g/6½-oz. jar artichoke pieces in olive oil, drained

120 g/4 oz. Parma ham (or prosciutto ham)

SERVES 4

Put a little swirl of ham on top of each piece of artichoke and skewer with a cocktail stick/toothpick.

Serve immediately. Easy peasy and ever so nice.

These tasty, pastry-free tartlets are great for everyone who loves the classic ham and egg combo, while the porcini mushrooms add a lovely depth of flavour.

TORTINE DI FUNGHI SELVATICI CON PROSCIUTTO DI PARMA
WILD MUSHROOM & PARMA HAM TARTLETS

20 g/scant 1 cup dried porcini mushrooms
180 g/6 oz. thinly sliced Parma ham
6 eggs
50 g/⅔ cup grated Parmesan
4–5 young fresh sage leaves, chopped

a small handful of chopped flat-leaf parsley
salt and black pepper, to season

a 6-cup muffin pan, lightly oiled

MAKES 6

Soak the porcini mushrooms in boiling water for 20 minutes or so, then drain and coarsely chop.

Preheat the oven to 150°C (300°F) Gas 2.

Carefully line the prepared muffin pan with the slices of ham, taking care not to leave any gaps that the egg might trickle through!

In a large mixing bowl, beat the eggs until smooth. Add the chopped mushrooms, remaining ingredients and season with salt and pepper. Divide the egg mixture between the lined pan holes and bake in the preheated oven for about 25 minutes, until the egg has set.

Remove from the oven, turn out and serve.

I spent a lovely part of my life working for a wonderful Swiss family in their home close to Geneva. The lady of the house had a Swiss dad and an Italian mum. She rarely ate meat, but she did adore Fegato alla Veneziana, which reminded her of her childhood in Italy. This dish typifies the best of traditional Venetian food. Don't skip the slow cooking of the onions – it's what makes the dish so special.

FEGATO ALLA VENEZIANA
CALVES' LIVER WITH ONIONS

6 tablespoons extra virgin olive oil
2 large onions, thinly sliced
50 g/3½ tablespoons butter
750 g/1⅔ lbs. calves' liver, thinly
    sliced
150 ml/⅔ cup Marsala wine
    (or white wine)
a handful of fresh sage
salt and black pepper, to season

SERVES 4-6

Pour 4 tablespoons of the oil into a large frying pan/ skillet and add the onions. Cook over a low heat for about 30 minutes, until they are melting and soft. Season with salt and pepper, then remove from the heat.

Heat the remaining oil and half of the butter together in a separate frying pan/skillet set over a high heat and cook the liver for 1 minute on each side. Remove from the pan and keep warm.

Pour the Marsala or white wine into the frying pan/ skillet and add the sage leaves. Allow to bubble for 2–3 minutes, then stir in the onions and the remaining butter. Arrange the liver in a serving dish, spoon over the onions and serve immediately.

Polpette make very popular cicchetti, usually served with a tomato sauce as I've done here. I think they're best served piping hot – but don't be surprised to find them served straight from the counter and cold in many of the Venetian bacari! This lovely recipe can be served with pasta as a main course, too. I would advise cooking a little of the meat mixture to check the seasoning, before forming it into balls – once they're formed and cooked, it's too late if you find them a little lacking in salt!

POLPETTE DI CARNE CON SALSA DI POMODORO
MEATBALLS WITH TOMATO SAUCE

1 medium onion, finely chopped
400 g/14 oz. good-quality finely minced/ground beef
200 g/7 oz. good-quality finely minced/ground pork
120 g/1¾ cups finely grated Parmesan
a small handful of fresh flat-leaf parsley, chopped
salt and black pepper, to season
4 tablespoons sunflower oil, for frying

TOMATO SAUCE
3–4 tablespoons extra virgin olive oil
1 onion, finely chopped
800 g/4 cups canned cherry tomatoes
1 scant teaspoon white sugar
a handful of freshly torn basil leaves
salt and black pepper, to season

SERVES 6-8

Preheat the oven to 180°C (350°F) Gas 4.

To make the meatballs, put the onion, minced/ground beef and minced/ground pork into a large mixing bowl and mix well. Add the Parmesan and parsley, and season with salt and pepper. Form the mixture into balls the size of a walnut and set aside.

To make the tomato sauce, heat the oil in a frying pan/skillet and cook the onion over a low heat for about 10 minutes, until softened but not coloured. Add the canned cherry tomatoes and sugar, and season to taste with salt and pepper. Let the mixture bubble for about 15 minutes, then add the basil. Cook for a further 10 minutes, until the sauce is thickened and glossy.

Heat the sunflower oil in a frying pan/skillet and fry the meatballs for 2–3 minutes on each side, until golden brown (I like to cook a small meatball first to taste and adjust the seasoning if necessary). Transfer them to a roasting pan and pour over the tomato sauce. Bake in the preheated oven for about 20 minutes, until the meatballs are cooked through.

Serve warm.

I'd be lying if I didn't admit that I've had the odd unpleasant crocchette in Venice. Unfortunately, some of the not-so-hot bacari do resort to buying in their cicchetti rather than making them in house. On top of that they serve them cold from the counter, so the result is disappointing, to say the least. However, these lovely light, crisp crocchette are poles apart from those dodgy freezer-to-fryer specimens. Smoky Scamorza cheese, salty speck, fresh rosemary and a crunchy Parmesan and polenta coating make these little treats irresistible. They're lovely with the Tomato Sauce served on page 46, but I love them most of all served alongside Mostarda di Cremona, a lovely concoction of candied fruit in a mustardy syrup that comes from the North of Italy and should be easy to find in good delis and Italian food stores.

CROCCHETTE DI PATATE, SPECK E RICOTTA AFFUMICATA
POTATO, SPECK & SMOKED RICOTTA CROCCHETTE

500 g/1 lb. 2 oz. floury potatoes
2 dried bay leaves
150 g/1⅓ cup grated Scamorza
    (smoked mozzarella)
100 g/¾ cup chopped speck ham
1 teaspoon finely chopped fresh
    rosemary
1 egg
salt and black pepper, to season
sunflower oil, for frying
lemon wedges and Mostarda di
    Cremona (jarred mixed mustard
    fruits), to serve (optional)

COATING
50 g/⅔ cup finely grated Parmesan
75 g/½ cup fine quick-cook polenta
    (I use Polenta Valsugana)

MAKES ABOUT 10

Boil the potatoes in a large saucepan of salted water with the bay leaves, until they are soft all the way through when tested with a metal skewer or the thin blade of a knife. Drain and leave until cold enough to handle comfortably. The exact cooking time will vary according to the size of potatoes used. Once they are cold, peel away the skin and coarsely grate into a large mixing bowl.

Add the grated Scamorza, speck and rosemary, and gently stir everything until it is evenly mixed. Add the egg, mix again and season the mixture with salt and pepper. Form the mixture into mini log shapes and (if you have time) pop them in the fridge for 30 minutes to firm up.

For the coating, mix the Parmesan and polenta together, then roll the logs in the mixture to coat them evenly.

Heat the sunflower oil in a deep saucepan to 190°C (375°F). Fry the crocchette until golden. Drain on paper towels.

Serve with lemon wedges and Mostarda di Cremona, if desired.

CROSTINI &
TRAMEZZINI

All'Arco is a tiny little gem of a bacari on the Ramo de L'Arco, quite close to the Rialto Market and a stone's throw away from the wonderful Cantina Do Mori. Amongst the many delights I've eaten there is a seemingly unassuming crostini topped only with Gorgonzola cheese and a single anchovy – and yet it was utterly sublime. In my version, I've taken the liberty of adding a little pickled radicchio/Italian chicory. It's a quick pickle that can be prepared in minutes and simply needs cooling rather than storing in sterilized glass jars. I think the lovely sweet and sour flavour with a hint of fennel seed makes it even better – a real cloud nine combo. More often than not, Venetian crostini bases are simply slices of baguette. I like to toast the slices on a griddle, or bake them in the oven with a little slick of olive oil to give them a lovely crunch that highlights the flavour of the topping even more.

CROSTINI DI GORGONZOLA E ACCIUGHE
GORGONZOLA & ANCHOVY CROSTINI

12 slices small baguette
3–4 tablespoons extra virgin olive oil
300 g/2½ cups Gorgonzola
12 canned anchovies

PICKLED RADICCHIO/ITALIAN CHICORY
300 ml/1¼ cups apple vinegar
1 generous tablespoon runny honey
1 teaspoon fennel seeds
1 small long radicchio/Italian chicory, sliced

MAKES 12

To pickle the radicchio/Italian chicory, pour the apple vinegar into a large saucepan and bring to the boil. Boil for a couple of minutes, then add the honey and fennel seeds. Turn the heat down and bubble for 5 minutes. Drop the sliced radicchio/Italian chicory into the vinegar, cook for 1 minute, then turn off the heat. After 4–5 minutes, remove the radicchio/Italian chicory and fennel seeds with a slotted spoon, transfer to a mixing bowl and cool.

Brush the baguette slices with the oil and toast on a hot griddle pan until golden (alternatively bake in a hot oven for 5 minutes or so).

Top each slice with a good dollop of Gorgonzola cheese and add a single anchovy. Garnish with the pickled radicchio/Italian chicory and serve.

Peas and mint make such a heavenly combination, especially on top of a crunchy crostini. I love to make them when peas are in season, but good-quality frozen ones are pretty good, too.

CROSTINI DI PISELLI E MENTA
PEA & MINT CROSTINI

10–12 slices baguette
60 ml/4 tablespoons extra virgin olive oil
1 garlic clove
250 g/1⅔ cups fresh peas (or 250 g/2 cups frozen peas)

a small handful of young fresh mint leaves, roughly chopped, plus extra to garnish
salt, to season
zest of 1 lemon, to garnish

MAKES 10–12

Preheat the oven to 180°C (350°F) Gas 4.

Brush the baguette slices with a little of the oil and place on a baking sheet. Cook in the preheated oven for about 10 minutes until golden and crisp. Remove from the oven and rub lightly with the garlic clove.

If you're using fresh peas, cook them in boiling salted water for about 3 minutes, drain and pop into a blender. If you're using frozen peas, simply defrost them and pop them straight into the blender. Add the remaining oil and whizz to a lightly textured purée. Remove from the blender and stir in the mint.

Form the pea mixture into neat quenelles using two teaspoons and top the crostini. Scatter with a little lemon zest and a few extra mint leaves and serve.

Most bacari serve some sort of crostini topped with salt cod. Soak the fish for 48 hours before blending, changing the water often. Laced with garlic and speckled with herbs, Baccalà con Aglio is a delight.

CROSTINI DI BACCALÀ CON AGLIO
SALT COD CROSTINI

500 g/1 lb. 2 oz. salt cod, soaked for 48 hours
570 ml/2¼ cups whole milk
2 fresh bay leaves
1 tablespoon black peppercorns
2 garlic cloves
120 ml/½ cup extra virgin olive oil, plus extra for brushing

a handful of fresh flat-leaf parsley, finely chopped
12 slices baguette, baked as left
salt and black pepper, to season

MAKES 12

Preheat the oven to 180°C (350°F) Gas 4.

Place the pre-soaked cod in a large saucepan and pour in the milk. Add the bay leaves, peppercorns, garlic and enough water to cover the fish. Set over a medium heat and simmer for 20 minutes or so, until just cooked. Remove the fish from the milk and strain out the bits and bobs, reserving the milk and the garlic.

Meanwhile, when the fish has cooled a little, flake it carefully into the bowl of a food processor or blender, taking care to remove the bones. Add half of the olive oil, a little of the reserved milk and the softened garlic and pulse, adding the remaining oil and as much milk as necessary, until the mixture has a similar thickness to that of creamy mashed potato. Stir in the parsley, adjust the seasoning and use it to top the crostini.

I can still picture the canal-front cicchetteria where I had a dish with a base made of polenta. Mixed with good-quality vegetable stock, butter and some Parmesan, and griddled until crisp, polenta makes a brilliant base for crostini. I like to add a slosh of Pastis (an aniseed-flavoured liqueur) before roasting the fennel to heighten its flavour. Don't skip the sprinkling of sugar and roast the crostini until caramel coloured.

CROSTINI DI POLENTA CON FINOCCHIO CARAMELLATO E GAMBERI
POLENTA CROSTINI WITH CARAMELIZED FENNEL & SHRIMP

juice of 2 lemons
2 bulbs of Florence fennel, trimmed
    and cut into wedges
2 teaspoons white sugar
50 ml/3½ tablespoons extra virgin
    olive oil, plus extra for frying
2 garlic cloves, finely chopped
zest and juice of ½ lemon
20 raw jumbo prawns/shrimp, peeled
    and deveined
salt and black pepper, to season
1 tablespoon chopped fresh chives
    (or a few fennel fronds), to garnish

POLENTA CROSTINI
500 ml/2 cups good-quality vegetable
    stock
125 g/¾ cup fine quick-cook polenta
    (I use Polenta Valsugana)
30 g/2 tablespoons butter
50 g/⅔ cup finely grated Parmesan

a baking sheet, oiled

MAKES 20

For the polenta crostini, heat the stock in a saucepan until boiling. Turn the heat down slightly and slowly add the polenta, stirring all the time. Continue to stir until the polenta is thick and smooth, and comes away from the sides of the pan. Remove from the heat and stir in the butter and Parmesan. Spoon onto the prepared baking sheet and spread out to about 1 cm/⅜ inch deep. Leave to set. When the polenta is completely cold, cut into circles about 3 cm/1¼ inches in diameter using a cookie cutter or the top of a small glass.

Preheat the oven to 190°C (375°F) Gas 5.

Fill a saucepan with water and add the juice of ½ lemon. Drop the wedges of fennel immediately into the acidulated water. Bring the water to the boil, turn the heat down and simmer for 10 minutes. Drain the fennel and lay it in a single layer on a baking sheet. Squeeze over the remaining lemon juice, scatter over the sugar and season. Roast for 25–30 minutes, until golden.

Meanwhile, bring a large saucepan of salted water to the boil. Mix the extra virgin olive oil, garlic, lemon zest and juice together in a large mixing bowl and season to taste. Drop the prawns/shrimp into the boiling water and cook for 2 minutes, until pink and lightly cooked. Lift them from the pan with a slotted spoon and drop them straight into the oil mixture. Stir and cool.

To assemble the crostini, brush the polenta bases with a little oil and cook on a hot griddle pan until golden. Top each with the caramelized fennel and a prawn/shrimp. Garnish with chopped chives or fennel fronds and serve.

TRAMEZZINI
VENETIAN TEA SANDWICHES

These dainty, crustless white sandwiches appear all over Venice in the bacari and coffee shops, and are always packed full of a moreish combination of ingredients.

HAM & EGG

4 eggs
3 tablespoons mayonnaise (see right)
6 thick slices white bread
200 g/1 cup Robiolino (or other buttery cream cheese)
6 slices cooked ham

MAKES 12

Bring a saucepan of water to the boil and gently drop in the eggs. Boil for 4 minutes. Remove from the heat and put the pan under cold running water for 3–4 minutes to halt the cooking. Peel the eggs, put in a bowl and chop them into small pieces or mash with a fork. Stir in enough mayonnaise to bind the egg without making the mixture sloppy.

Spread the bread with Robiolino, on one side only. Arrange the ham over half of the slices and top with the egg. Lay the remaining slices on top, remove the crusts and cut into elegant fingers. Serve.

CHICKEN & MAYO

2 cooked chicken breasts, diced
1 small radicchio/Italian chicory, thinly sliced
3 tablespoons extra virgin olive oil
1 tablespoon balsamic vinegar
6 thick slices white bread
200 g/1 cup Robiolino (or other buttery cream cheese)

MAYONNAISE
1 egg
2–3 tablespoons white wine vinegar
1 generous teaspoon Dijon mustard
200 ml/¾ cup sunflower oil

MAKES 12

For the mayonnaise, put the egg, vinegar and mustard into the bowl of a blender. Add a pinch of salt and whizz to combine. With the motor running, slowly drizzle in the oil, until the mixture starts to thicken and the oil is incorporated.

Put the chicken in a bowl and add enough mayonnaise to bind it without making it sloppy. Season.

Put the radicchio/Italian chicory into a separate bowl. Drizzle with extra virgin olive oil and balsamic vinegar.

Spread the bread with Robiolino on one side only. Spread the chicken over half of the slices and top with the radicchio/Italian chicory. Lay the remaining slices on top, remove the crusts and cut into fingers. Serve.

SALMON & CREAM CHEESE

6 thick slices white bread
200 g/1 cup Robiolino (or other buttery cream cheese)
150 g/5½ oz. thinly sliced smoked salmon

MAKES 12

Spread the bread with soft cheese, on one side only. Arrange the smoked salmon over half of the slices. Lay the remaining slices on top, remove the crusts and cut into elegant fingers. Serve.

In the corner of the Campo Cesare Battisti, there is a wonderful little place called Al Mercà. Little more than a hole in the wall, it has a huge following of locals and tourists in the know. I fell in love with the small but perfectly formed, generously filled panini.

LITTLE CHEESE & HAM TOASTIES FLORIAN STYLE

6 large slices of white bread
200 g/1 cup Robiolino (or other buttery cream cheese)
6 thin slices cooked ham
150 g/5½ oz. Asiago (or other mild Italian cheese), grated
50 g/3½ tablespoons butter, softened

MAKES 12

Preheat the oven to 190°C (375°F) Gas 5. Spread the bread with Robiolino on one side. Lay ham over three of the slices and top with the grated Asiago cheese. Sandwich together with the remaining slices of bread and spead the outer sides with butter.

Put on a baking sheet and bake in the preheated oven for 10–15 minutes, until golden.

Remove from the oven and cut off the crusts. Eat quite a few of the crusts whilst cutting the sandwiches into small squares. Thread two sandwiches onto each skewer and serve immediately.

ROASTED VEGETABLE & MOZZARELLA CLUBS

2 small courgettes/zucchini, sliced
1 small aubergine/eggplant, sliced
3 tablespoons extra virgin olive oil
home-dried tomatoes (see page 31)
125 g/4½ oz. firm mozzarella
a small bunch of fresh basil
a handful of fresh rocket/arugula
9 thick slices white bread
200 g/1 cup Robiolino (or other buttery cream cheese)
50 g/3½ tablespoons butter, softened
salt and black pepper, to season

MAKES 12

Preheat the oven to 190°C (375°F) Gas 5. Put the courgette/zucchini and aubergine/eggplant into a large mixing bowl and toss with the oil. Heat a griddle pan until hot, and griddle the slices until just cooked but still firm. Remove from the heat, season and leave to cool.

Spread half of the bread with soft cheese. Layer up the vegetables with the home-dried tomatoes, slices of mozzarella and basil leaves, placing an extra slice of bread in the centre.

Spread the outside slices of bread with butter and put on a baking sheet. Bake for 10–15 minutes, until the bread is toasted and golden. Cut off the crusts, then cut into small triangles to serve.

MINI PANINI

12 mini ciabatta rolls (see Note), sliced

FILLING SUGGESTIONS
salsciccia picante e robiola (pepperoni sausage and cream cheese)
Gorgonzola dolce e noci (Gorgonzola and walnut)
coppa di Parma (cured pork loin)
manzo fume, crema di asparagi e rucola (smoked beef, creamed asparagus and rocket/arugula)
verdure Mediterranea grigliate (grilled Mediterranean vegetables)

MAKES 12

Top the ciabatta bases with your chosen filling and lay the lids on top. Thread onto a small skewer to hold everything together and serve.

Note: if you can't find mini ciabatta rolls, prepare the Pizzette Dough on page 18 and form balls before baking.

BEVANDE

It is said in Venice that the Spritz isn't just a drink, it's a way of life. It would be almost impossible to visit Venice without sitting in the sunshine sipping on one of these coral-coloured delights. Use either Aperol or Campari for a classic Spritz – Aperol is slightly sweeter and less alcoholic, while Campari gives a drier result. Recipes vary – sometimes white wine is used, sometimes Prosecco. Some advocate equal quantities of Prosecco or wine to Campari or Aperol and sparkling water. Others use a 3:2:1 ratio – three parts Prosecco or wine to two parts Campari or Aperol and one part sparkling water. Campari-based drinks make great aperitivi – the slight bitterness stimulates the appetite. Gin fans watch out for the Negroni, it is very addictive! The pomegranate-spiked Tintoretto is a pretty and delicious cocktail from the legendary Venetian institution Caffè Florian in St. Mark's Square.

NEGRONI

crushed ice
180 ml/¾ cup Campari
180 ml/¾ cup gin
60 ml/¼ cup Cinzano Rosso
orange slices, to serve

MAKES 4

Fill four long glasses with crushed ice. Divide the Campari between the glasses, then the gin. Add the Cinzano Rosso and stir.

Drop a slice of orange into each glass and serve.

SPRITZ

ice cubes
200 ml/¾ cup Campari (or Aperol)
600 ml/2½ cups Prosecco (or white wine)
300–400 ml/1¼–1½ cups sparkling water

MAKES 4

Put lots of cubed (never crushed) ice into four large, chilled wine glasses. Divide the Campari (or Aperol) and Prosecco (or white wine) between the glasses, then top up with sparkling water.

Serve immediately.

TINTORETTO

140 ml/½ cup pomegranate juice
600 ml/2½ cups Prosecco

MAKES 4

Pour the pomegranate juice into four chilled Champagne flutes, then top up with Prosecco.

Serve at once.

Left to right: Spritz, Tintoretto, Negroni

CHAMPAGNE COCKTAILS

Perhaps the most famous of all Venetian cocktails, the Bellini was invented by Giuseppe Cipriani at the celebrated Harry's Bar in Venice around 70 years ago. It's a mixture of fresh white peach juice and Prosecco. To stay true to the original flavour (and enjoy the best cocktail), only white peaches (not yellow) will do. And absolutely no canned peaches! Please! The secret is to adapt your Bellini to the changing seasons – better to try a different fruit entirely than to make a poor cocktail using under-ripe fruit, pasteurized fruit juices or anything from a can. Keep the ingredients and glasses as cold as possible. The Harry's Bar formula is about three to four parts sparkling wine to one part peach purée. Why change the stuff that legends are made of? Cin! Cin!

CLASSIC

40 ml/3 tablespoons freshly made white peach purée
480 ml/2 cups Prosecco

MAKES 4

Pour the peach purée into the chilled Champagne flutes. Pour in the Prosecco and stir gently.

Serve immediately.

STRAWBERRY & BASIL

5 ripe strawberries
1 teaspoon white sugar
a small handful of fresh basil leaves
120 ml/½ cup Prosecco

MAKES 1

Whizz the strawberries and sugar together in a blender to make a purée. Pour the purée into a jug/pitcher, add a little of the Prosecco and the basil. Bash with a blunt object until lots of flavour has been released. Pour the mixture through the strainer into a chilled glass. Pour over the remaining Prosecco and stir gently. Serve immediately.

PEAR

200 ml/¾ cup pear purée
480 ml/2 cups Prosecco

MAKES 4

Pour the pear purée into the chilled glasses. Pour in the Prosecco and stir gently.

Serve immediately.

Left to right: Pear Bellini, Strawberry & Basil Bellini, Classic Bellini

INDEX

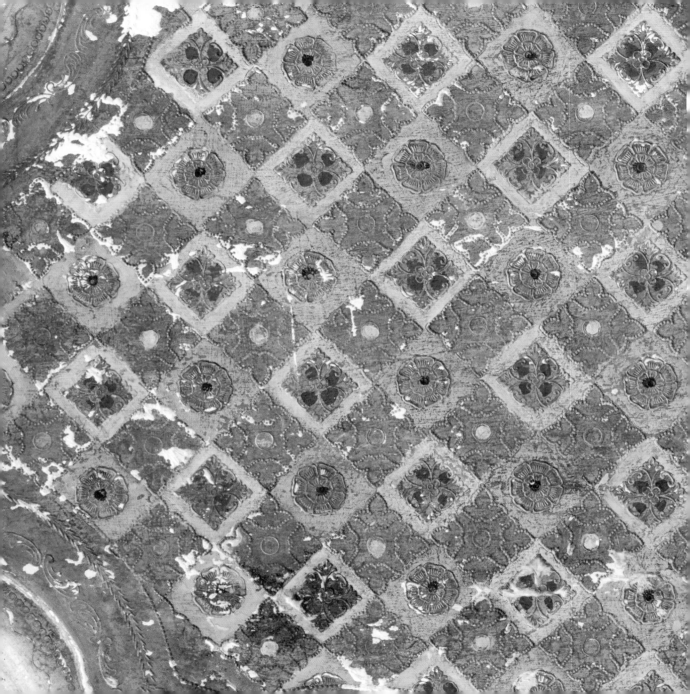